Mo
9/03
State

ECO-CAREERS

A guide to jobs in the environmental field

John Hamilton

Published by Abdo & Daughters, 4940 Viking Dr., Suite 622, Edina, Minnesota 55435.

Library bound edition distributed by Rockbottom Books,
Pentagon Tower, P.O. Box 36036, Minneapolis, Minnesota 55435.

Edited By: Sue L. Hamilton
Cover Photo: Stock Market
Inside Photos: The Bettmann Archive, Peter Arnold, Inc., Dayton Hudson Corp., Northern States Power Company.

Library of Congress Cataloging-in-Publication Data
Hamilton, John, 1954–
    ECO-careers: a guide to jobs in the environmental field / written by John Hamilton.
            p.   cm – (Target earth)
    Includes index
    Summary: Examines twelve different jobs in which people work to preserve our environment including agronomist, environmental lawyer, teacher, and toxicologist.
    ISBN 1-56239-209-3
    1. Environmental sciences–Vocational guidance–Juvenile literature. [1. Environmental sciences–Vocational guidance 2. Vocational guidance.] I. Title. II. Series.
GE60.H36   1993
363.7' 0023' 73–dc20   93-7601
                                                        CIP
                                                        AC

 Thanks to the trees from which this recycled paper was first made.

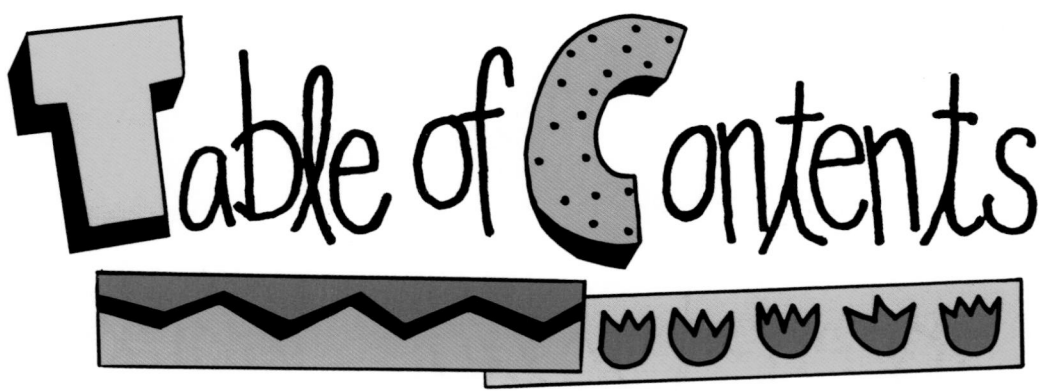

Table of Contents

Chapter 1

Green-Collar Workers

In April 1990, this country celebrated the 20th anniversary of Earth Day. With the celebration came a renewed awareness and interest in protecting our fragile environment. Back in 1970, when the original Earth Day was celebrated, being an environmentalist was a novelty, something most "normal" people didn't think of doing. Today, all that has changed. Our society has found a huge amount of new energy directed toward saving the environment. With an increase in attention from the news media, plus a large number of new, stricter laws taking effect, environmentalism seems to be on everyone's mind these days. Being an "environmentalist" is no longer a dirty word. To the contrary, more and more people today are seeking employment in environmental work.

To have a job "working with the environment" can mean many things to many people. Whether you're an engineer designing new, cleaner smokestacks, a park ranger guiding tourists through unspoiled national parkland, or a teacher showing school kids how to recycle their garbage, you've got an eco-career. You have to decide where your interests are, and how you want to use your skills. Your choices are many.

Choosing an environmental career doesn't mean you have to have a strict formal education. Most people who want an eco-career will get at least a four-year degree from a college, usually in the hard sciences like biology or engineering. But this isn't always necessary.

While many eco-jobs require such a degree, an informal education is almost as important as what you'll gain from college. College teaches you how to learn. It's how you use that learning that counts. The work you do on the job will determine how far you go in your field. With everything changing so rapidly in the environmental field, you never stop learning.

The following list of eco-careers is only a small sampling of jobs available to those with an interest in the environment. The rewards of an eco-career are many, especially if you love the outdoors and the natural environment.

Working in a field you truly enjoy is a rare thing these days. Getting paid for doing what you love is an added bonus. And perhaps most importantly, by focusing your work on the environment, you'll help make the world a better place for all of us to live.

Chapter 2

Agronomist

The chief duty of an agronomist (those working in agriculture) is to find better ways of planting, raising, and harvesting crops so that farmers can get more out of their land. Today, agronomists are putting a lot of thought and effort into "low-input" agriculture, which basically means planting crops with a minimum of fertilizers, pesticides and intensive plowing. Today more and more grocery shoppers are demanding "pure" and "natural" foods. It's the agronomist's job to find ways to grow crops that aren't tainted with too many pesticides and chemicals, yet are still economical for farmers to grow.

In addition to working with crops, agronomists also deal with lawn care and landscaping. It's also their job to find ways of reclaiming land that's been drastically damaged, such as toxic waste dumps.

For more information, write to: American Society of Agronomy, 677 South Segoe Rd., Madison, WI 53711.

Agronomist Dr. R. Betz examines soil samples.

Chapter 3

Air Quality Scientist

Air quality scientists are meteorologists who work in the environmental area. They try to understand the Earth's atmosphere and how air pollution behaves when it gets into our air. For example, building taller smokestacks helps keep air pollution away from our cities, but where does the pollution go? An air quality scientist will use computer models of weather patterns to predict which areas downwind from heavy industry or automobile traffic will be affected by air pollution and acid rain. If there is an accidental toxic leak, like a cloud of chlorine from a storage tank, the air quality scientist will predict which communities need to evacuate to escape the deadly cloud.

Air quality scientists also analyze samples from smokestacks and automobiles, set up and operate air quality samplers in cities and industrial sites, and evaluate how well pollution-control equipment is working. Many air quality scientists also work on big, worldwide issues like ozone depletion, acid rain, and global warming.

For more information, write to: National Association of Environmental Professionals, P.O. Box 15210, Alexandria, VA 22309-0210.

Air quality scientist Janet Anderson is responsible for her utility company's air, soil, and vegetation monitoring programs.

Chapter 4

Ecologist

Ecology is the study of systems of living things, which we call eco-systems. Today, as we try to preserve wildlife habitats and slow animal extinction, there is a growing need for people with technical skills in ecology. When developers wish to build on certain kinds of land, or the government tries to decide how to use public land (recreational or commercial), they often call on an ecologist. Ecologists collect data and take field samples, trying to understand each ecosystem. When they understand how all the parts of an ecosystem work, how they are interconnected, they can then decide which parts can be safely put to use by humans without destroying the whole ecosystem. It's a very important job, because one mistake can wipe out a whole ecosystem.

Ecologists usually specialize in one of several areas. For instance, one ecologist might be an expert in forests, trying to learn the fragile balance between the trees, the plants, and animals. Another ecologist may be a specialist in swamps and wetlands. Each ecosystem has its own special needs, and must be fully understood before humans start developing it. It's the ecologist's job to make sure we use our land wisely without wrecking things for future generations.

For more information, contact: Ecological Society of America, Center for Environmental Studies, Arizona State University, Tempe, AZ 85187.

Ecologist Marsha Carey.

Chapter 5

Environmental Geologist

The quality of our drinking water is something most people no longer take for granted. With the rise in toxic waste dumps, landfills, and other sources of contamination, our drinking water supplies have never been more threatened. Environmental geologists, or hydrogeologists, analyze how badly groundwater, and the soil above it, is con-taminated with toxic waste or other poisons, like pesticides, or even radioactivity. They bore small holes into the ground, called soil borings, to get samples of the ground and water at various depths. Then they take these samples to a laboratory and analyze them, looking for contamination.

Environmental geologists often develop computer programs to predict how badly ground water is contaminated, and how long it will take to clean it up. They also use sensitive instruments in the field, like ground-penetrating radar, to search for buried drums or tanks of toxic waste. When these kinds of things are discovered, they must be dug up and disposed of properly. The environmental geologist is usually on hand to supervise the disposal to make sure the ground doesn't get even more contaminated.

A related career is that of water quality technologist. These people usually work for industries that emit waste water back into the ecosystem, like paper mills or food processors. They also work for city water and waste treatment plants. Their job is to make sure the water put back into the ecosystem is as clean as possible without violating government clean-water laws.

For more information, contact: Association of Ground Water Scientists and Engineers, 6375 Riverside Drive, Dublin, OH 43017.

Chuck Donkers is an environmental geologist for Northern States Power Company in Minneapolis, Minnesota.

Chapter 6

Environmental Lawyer

Environmental laws are especially complex. During the last 10 to 20 years, Congress and the states have passed thousands of new laws aimed at cleaning the environment and getting tough with companies and individuals who pollute. The U.S. government has many full-time lawyers working on bringing polluters to justice. These lawyers work for such agencies as the Environmental Protection Agency, and are backed by the F.B.I. To protect themselves from huge fines, many corporations hire their own lawyers to make sure they stay within the law. All of this activity has made lawyers who specialize in environmental law especially sought after.

Corporate work is only one area for environmental lawyers. Another is preparing environmental impact statements that are required today for most new major construction projects. And of course there's always work to be done saving forests and animals from development and extinction. Many non-profit (or private) organizations have lawyers on staff who work on a wide variety of issues, from pollution control to wildlife preservation on behalf of their members. Environmental lawyers, it seems, are needed in just about every major area of the eco-movement.

For more information, contact: Environmental Law Institute, 1616 P Street N.W., Washington, D.C. 20036.

Carol Garland Wiessner is a staff lawyer for the Minnesota Center for Environmental Advocacy, a non-profit environmental group.

Chapter 7

Forester

Foresters work with, as you might guess, trees and forests. They are responsible for making sure our forest land is used in the best way possible, whether for wilderness, parkland or industry (mainly logging). A forester will learn, in a particular section of forest, how many trees there are and what kind. From this knowledge, decisions can be made about harvesting logs.

Foresters also must know how to protect a forest ecosystem. For example, if too many trees are cut down in too big an area, water cycles get disrupted. Topsoil erosion makes it very hard to grow new trees. Foresters also assess the damage done from air pollution and acid rain. They are also very knowledgeable about identifying and treating various kinds of tree diseases.

When fires spread through forests, it is the forester who tries to figure out how the fire will behave and how best to fight it. A forester understands the role of fire in an ecosystem and how it can also be used as a tool to make forests stronger.

For more information, contact: The American Forestry Association, 1516 P Street N.W., Washington, D.C. 20005.

Foresters identify and treat many kinds of tree diseases.

Chapter 8

Oceanographer

Obviously not all eco-careers are tied to the land. If spending parts of your job on a ship appeals to you, then consider the career of oceanographer. Oceanographers study the oceans and seas. They try to understand marine plants and animals, the way waves and currents affect our coastal areas, and the geography of the deep ocean bottom. Oceanographers may spend quite a bit of time on research vessels (including submarines), collecting data to be analyzed at laboratories back on shore. The results of their studies help us understand the impact of the dumping of industrial waste and sewer runoff, tell us where oil and other mineral deposits lie, and how our actions affect marine life, (such as whales and dolphin, fish, and underwater plant life).

With the increased interest in using the seas for economic development, oceanographers are now in demand by government and private industry. Competition for these jobs can be intense, but if science, the environment, and life on the high seas appeals to you, becoming an oceanographer may be just the ticket.

For more information, contact: Oceanic Society, 218 D Street S.E., Washington, D.C. 20003.

Capt. Jacques Cousteau aboard his ship Calypso.

Chapter 9

Park Ranger

Who hasn't dreamed of someday becoming a ranger in a national park? If you like working in the great outdoors, and you like working with people, then this is the job for you—if you can get one. Competition for park ranger jobs in the national parks is intense because there are so few jobs for so many people. Luckily, there are other jobs waiting in state parks or recreation areas. So though you may not be tagging bears in Yellowstone, you might instead be checking fishermen for proper licenses at a city lake, talking to interested citizens at a local wetlands preserve about respect for nature, or patrolling a state park campground and investigating a crime.

The range of work for park rangers is quite large, and their backgrounds are just as varied. You'll need at least a bachelor's degree, a good knowledge of conservation law, and a desire to work with people. People with law enforcement backgrounds are also in growing demand because of rising crime rates in our public parks.

For more information, contact: National Recreation and Park Association, 3101 Park Center Drive, Alexandria, VA 22302.

Paul Sundberg is a park ranger for the Minnesota DNR-Forestry Division.

Chapter 10

Teacher

School teachers can have an important impact on our society's environmental awareness. While there are few who teach strictly in the environmental area, many teachers include eco-issues as part of their classes in other broader subjects like biology, geography, or social studies.

Teachers introduce students to important eco-issues like recycling and conservation. Field trips to parks and nature centers, recycling facilities, or wetland preserves often inspire students to pursue eco-careers of their own. Instilling environmental values in their students is perhaps a teacher's most important job. Well-taught students are an investment in our future.

For more information, contact: North American Association for Environmental Education, P.O. Box 400, Troy, OH 45373.

Harold Tuttle, Environmental Teacher of the Year in New Hamphire. Tuttle helped organize "Greenkids," an environmental activist group formed by a 6th grade class at Lafayette Regional School.

Chapter 11

Toxicologist

Environmental toxicologists are the Sherlock Holmes' of environmental work. Their job is to find out if people are getting sick because of a chemical, and where that chemical came from. Using their knowledge of biology and chemistry, toxicologists also try to find out if human exposure to chemicals emitted by industry should be of concern to people living nearby. It's their job to find out how much toxic substances human activity is allowed to put into our air and water. Industry often hires toxicologists to test their products to make sure they are safe.

Sometimes many people in a neighborhood get sick and we don't know why. A toxicologist might be called in to find out if something in the environment is causing the illness. Through their work, toxicologists sometimes find links between certain diseases and substances we used to think were safe. For example, we now know that there is a link between lung cancer and asbestos, thanks to the work of dedicated toxicologists.

For more information, contact: Society of Toxicology, 1101 Fourteenth Street N.W., Washington, D.C. 20005.

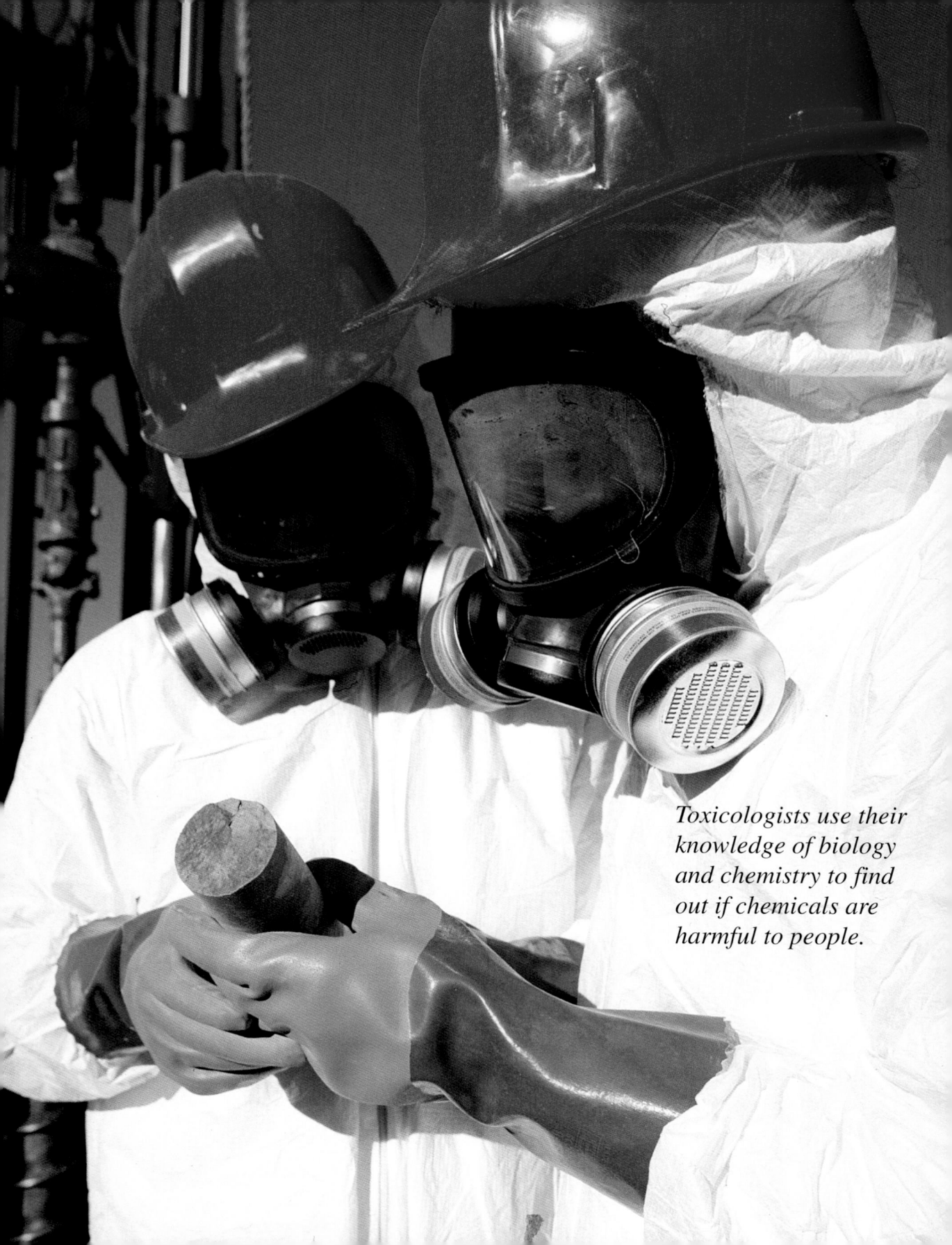

Toxicologists use their knowledge of biology and chemistry to find out if chemicals are harmful to people.

Chapter 12

Writer/Photographer

Many writers and photographers (both still and video) combine their communications skills with a love for the outdoors by specializing in environmental issues. The work changes with each assignment, and the chance to meet many different people in the environmental field can be rewarding.

Becoming a writer or photographer who specializes in environmental issues is a good example of an eco-career that doesn't necessarily require a degree in the hard sciences. But don't let that fool you. Successful communications professionals do a lot of research on their topics, ranging from searching through libraries, interviewing top people in the environmental field, and going out on location to report on environmental disasters firsthand. Those with technical backgrounds know how to ask the right questions to bring back stories their readers and viewers can understand.

For more information, contact: National Association of Professional Environmental Communicators, P.O. Box 06 8352, Chicago, IL 60606-8352.

Environmental writer and photographer Alex MacLean takes aerial photos from his plane.

Glossary

Acid rain

When rain (or snow, sleet or hail) contains a high level of sulfuric or nitric acids, it falls to the ground as "acid rain." Acid rain is produced when sulfur dioxide in the air (together with chemicals called nitrogen oxides) combine with moisture in the air. Acid rain can contaminate drinking water, damage plants and aquatic life, and erode buildings and monuments. Automobile exhausts and the burning of high-sulfur industrial fuels are thought to be the main causes.

Asbestos

A kind of mineral (called a fibrous silicate) that is resistant to acid and fire. It's used in such things as firefighting equipment, brake linings, and insulation. Studies have shown that asbestos particles in the air can cause lung cancer and the lung disease asbestosis.

Atmosphere

The mixture of gases and other substances surrounding the Earth. The atmosphere is composed mainly of nitrogen (78.09%), oxygen (20.95%), argon (0.93%), carbon dioxide (0.03%), and minute traces of neon, helium, methane, krypton, hydrogen, xenon, and ozone.

CFCs

CFCs (Chlorofluorocarbons) are a group of chemical compounds that contain the elements carbon, chlorine, fluorine, and sometimes hydrogen. They are found in refrigerators and air conditioners and are used to make plastics and other solutions.

Chlorine

Chlorine is a greenish-yellow, poisonous, gaseous element with a disagreeable, suffocating odor. Chlorine is a part of many different kinds of compounds (combination of chemicals). It's used in water purification, as a disinfectant and antiseptic, and in pesticides. Many poison gases contain chlorine. In medicine, chlorine is used in chloroform and chloral-hydrate.

Erosion

The way in which the Earth's surface is constantly worn away, usually because of running water, waves, glaciers or wind. The erosion of farmland topsoil is a big problem, especially in the United States. Ways to combat erosion include reforestation, terracing, and special plowing techniques.

Extinction

When a plant or animal species is completely wiped out, never to be seen again.

Global Warming (Greenhouse Effect)

The Earth is surrounded by a layer of invisible gases (the atmosphere). When the sun's rays shine down, much of the heat is trapped by these gases, acting much like the glass in a greenhouse. This is good, because we need heat to survive. But human activity through the burning of fossil fuels (coal, oil, gas, etc.) and deforestation has added increased amounts of gases like carbon dioxide and methane to the atmosphere. Many scientists believe these extra gases will heat up the Earth even more. An increase in atmospheric carbon dioxide of 10% over the past century makes some scientists predict a long-term warming of our climate.

Groundwater

Groundwater is water under the Earth's surface, between saturated soil and rock, that supplies wells and springs. Vast underground systems of groundwater are also called aquifers.

Ozone

Ozone is the most chemically active form of oxygen. It has a fresh, penetrating odor, and can often be smelled right after a thunderstorm. Most ozone is formed in the ozone layer of the atmosphere. The ozone layer keeps some of the sun's rays, which can be harmful to life, from reaching the Earth's surface. Scientists fear that some pollutants, like CFCs, are thinning the ozone layer, which could mean more of the sun's ultraviolet rays will reach us, causing damage to animals and plants.

Ozone also occurs at ground level. As motor vehicles speed along roads and highways, a witch's brew of gases spews from their exhaust pipes. Under the influence of sunlight, these gases undergo a series of chemical reactions. As a result, smog—which contains ozone—is formed. Ground-level ozone is harmful to plants and animals—including people.

Toxic Waste

Toxic wastes are often made in factories as a byproduct, and include heavy metals (like mercury, lead, and cadmium), certain hydrocarbons, and other poisons. Such substances are usually sealed in metal drums and deposited underground or in the ocean, but the containers often corrode and leak, polluting the land and water supply. Common household chemicals (cleaning products, paint, paint thinners, etc.) also are considered toxic waste when dumped in the trash. These household hazardous wastes must be disposed of properly.

Index

TARGET EARTH™ COMMITMENT

At Target, we're committed to the environment. We show this commitment not only through our own internal efforts but also through the programs we sponsor in the communities where we do business.

Our commitment to children and the environment began when we became the Founding International Sponsor for Kids for Saving Earth, a non-profit environmental organization for kids. We helped launch the program in 1989 and supported its growth to three-quarters of a million club members in just three years.

Our commitment to children's environmental education led to the development of an environmental curriculum called Target Earth,™ aimed at getting kids involved in their education and in their world.

In addition, we worked with Abdo & Daughters Publishing to develop the Target Earth™ Earthmobile, and environmental science library on wheels that can be used in libraries, or rolled from classroom to classroom.

Target believes that the children are our future and the future of our planet. Through education, they will save the world!

TARGET®

Minneapolis-based Target Stores is an upscale discount department store chain of 517 stores in 33 states coast-to-coast, and is the largest division of Dayton Hudson Corporation, one of the nation's leading retailers.